VEGA

PLANT-BASED SNACK RECIPES

Easy & Affordable Recipes for Healthy & Delicious Vegan Snacks!

By Braden O'Connor

INTRODUCTION 6
HEALTH BENEFITS OF FOLLOWING A VEGAN DIET 6
1. A vegan diet lowers the risk of stroke and numerous heart-related ailments..6
2. A vegan diet lowers the risk of acquiring and/or premature onset of numerous gastrointestinal ailments. 8
3. A vegan diet helps lower the risk and/or lessen symptoms of gastrointestinal cancer. 8
4. A vegan diet is a valuable tool in Type II diabetes management. 9
5. A vegan diet helps lower the risk and/or lessen symptoms of 2 types of arthritis...9
6. A vegan diet is a valuable tool in weight loss management.....10

A FEW THINGS TO REMEMBER BEFORE STARTING A VEGAN DIET...11
CONVERSION CHART..16
CHAPTER 1: BEVERAGES..17
CHILLED OR COLD DRINKS 17
Water Infusions...17
Apples and Carrots in Cinnamon Water 17
Blueberry and Citrus Infusion 19
Citrusy Basil and Strawberry Infusion 20
Ginger and Mango in Citrus Infusion 21
Shaved Fruits and Vegetables Infusion 22
Red Fruits Infusion 23

Power Juices...24
Apple-Pineapple Juice 24
Berries Power Juice 25
Carrot Power Juice 26
Pineapple and Papaya Power Juice.......................................27
Orange Colored Power Juice...28
Pineapple with Greens Power Juice......................................29
Tomato and Vegetable Power Juice......................................30

Shakes and Smoothies..31
ABC (Almond Milk, Berries, and Cashew Nuts) Shake 31
Apple Pie Shake...32
Blueberry, Strawberry and Flaxseed Shake..........................33
Chocolate Banana Shake 34
Coconut Salad Shake 35
Dill and Cucumber Smoothie..36
Fruity Green Smoothie..37
Walnut Smoothie 38

HOT OR WARM DRINKS 39
　Herbal Infusions (Caffeine-Free) 39
　　Apples and Chamomile Herbal Infusion 39
　　Berry and Lemon Herbal Infusion 40
　　Citrus and Peppermint Herbal Infusion 41
　　Forest Leaves Herbal Infusion 42
　　Fruity Ginger Herbal Infusion 43
　　Lavender and Mint Herbal Infusion 44
　　Raspberry Herbal Infusion 45

CHAPTER 2: SWEETS 46

NO-BAKE SWEETS 46
　Chocolate Chip Granola Bars 46
　Chewy "Walmond" Bars 48
　Sweet Banana Nut Bars 50
　Banana and Berry Sweetened Oats with Coconut Milk 52
　Boiled Plantains 54
　Brownies in Mugs 55
　Coconut and Jackfruit Flapjacks 57
　Elvis' Tricked Out Grilled Peanut Butter Sandwich 59
　Plantain Meal with Tropical Fruits Salad 61
　Spiced Poached Pears in White Wine 63
　Strawberry Flax Seed Jam 65

BAKED SWEETS 66
　Homemade Coconut Butter on Homemade Vegan Rye Bread 66
　Raspberry Glazed Almond Cupcakes 69
　Vegan Chocolate Cupcakes with Ginger & Orange 72
　Twice-Baked Sweet Potatoes and Purple Yam 75
　Hazelnut & Olive Oil Shortbread 77
　Peanut Butter & Jam Cookies 79

CHAPTER 3: SAVORY SNACKS 81

NO-BAKE SAVORY SNACKS 81
　Citrus-Flavored Kebab 81
　Grilled Corn with Coconut Butter 83
　Savory Veggie Fritters 84
　Homemade Hummus 86
　Simple & Savory Guacamole 88

BAKED SAVORY SNACKS 90
　Homemade Tortillas 90
　Baked Tortilla Chips 92
　Healthy Crispy Crackers 94

Spiced Potatoes and Sweet Potatoes 96
Deconstructed Pesto on Instant Sourdough Pizza 98
Squash Flower Pizza 101
Cheesy Kale Chips 103
Spicy Roasted Chickpeas 105
Easy Fluffy Vegan Rolls 107
Spinach & Sesame Crackers 109

Legal Disclaimer

The information provided herein is stated to be truthful and consistent, in that any liability, in terms of inattention or otherwise, by any usage or abuse of any policies, processes, or directions contained within is the solitary and utter responsibility of the recipient reader. Under no circumstances will any legal responsibility or blame be held against the publisher for any reparation, damages, or monetary loss due to the information herein, either directly or indirectly.

This document is geared towards providing exact and reliable information in regards to the topic and issue covered. The publication is sold with the idea that the publisher is not required to render accounting, officially permitted, or otherwise, qualified services. If advice is necessary, legal or professional, a practiced individual in the profession should be ordered.

The information herein is offered for informational purposes solely, and is universal as so. The presentation of the information is without contract or any type of guarantee assurance.

The trademarks that are used are without any consent, and the publication of the trademark is without permission or backing by the trademark owner. All trademarks and brands within this book are for clarifying purposes only and are the owned by the owners themselves, not affiliated with this document.

© Copyright 2016 by Braden O'Connor – All rights reserved.

Introduction

Health Benefits of Following a Vegan Diet

A vegan diet subscribes to the practice of consuming only plant-based food items and drinks. It discourages the use of animal-based products and by-products, including dairy (from milk producing animals,) eggs (from fish and poultry,) insects (and insect by-products, e.g. honey from bees,) and of course, meat (fresh, frozen, dried, or processed red and white meat, including seafood.)

Some people follow such a diet for ethical reasons (upholding animal rights.) Others subscribe to this for environmental concerns (fighting against mass meat production.) However, this particular eating regimen is also gaining more followers because of its numerous health benefits. Here are 6 of the most prevalent ones:

1. A vegan diet lowers the risk of stroke and numerous heart-related ailments.

Following a diet high in animal fat and protein leaves fatty deposits (called plaques) that build up and block arteries and veins. This hampers blood circulation, and prevents certain organs from acquiring ample supply of life-sustaining glucose and oxygen. To compensate, the heart automatically works overtime. It pumps blood at a higher-than-normal pressure (hence the term, high blood pressure.) Unfortunately, this process also speeds up the flow of fat that is already in the blood. This process congests more arteries and veins.

Chronic episodes of high blood pressure increase the risk of stroke, wherein plaque buildup effectively stops blood from reaching certain areas of the brain.

This can likewise lead to carotid artery disease (narrowing or blockage of carotid arteries found in the neck area,) coronary artery disease (*artherosclerosis* or blockage of arteries around/near the heart,) coronary heart disease (narrowing or blockage of arteries within the heart itself,) and peripheral artery disease (narrowing of arteries in the arms, legs, or other vital organs that supply blood to the heart.)

It should be noted that these conditions necessitate immediate medical intervention to prevent premature demise, or permanent/progressive loss of limbs and organ function.

2. A vegan diet lowers the risk of acquiring and/or premature onset of numerous gastrointestinal ailments.

It is said that animal protein is tougher on the digestive system than plant-based food items. Combined with high consumption of processed food and drinks that damage stomach and intestinal lining, an unhealthy meat-based diet triggers: bloating, flatulence, indigestion, and stomach cramps.

Other potentially life-threatening conditions triggered by this condition includes: Crohn's disease, diverticulitis, fecal impaction, gallstone pancreatitis, GERD or gastro-esophageal reflux disease, IBS or irritable bowel syndrome, and ulcerative colitis to name a few.

3. A vegan diet helps lower the risk and/or lessen symptoms of gastrointestinal cancer.

One prevailing thought in bowel, colon, stomach, and rectal cancer treatment is that: a high fiber diet lessens the possibility of cancerous polyps developing in the mucous lining of the digestive tract and intestinal walls. Not only does fiber move food quickly through the system, but it also expels toxins out of the body before these negatively affect surrounding tissues.

Though more research is needed to prove this point, some health care providers claim that a high plant-based diet also lessens risk/symptoms of other forms of cancer, like: bladder, brain, kidney, ovarian, pancreatic, prostate, skin, and thyroid.

4. A vegan diet is a valuable tool in Type II diabetes management.

Fresh produce, (particularly fruits and vegetables) and dried grains (dark colored grains, beans, legumes, and pulses) contain whole, rigid plant cells. When consumed, these break down at a slower rate as compared to simple carbohydrates found in sugars and most processed food.

For type II diabetics, who produce insulin hormones that inefficiently break down simple carbs, consuming whole food keeps blood sugar at manageable levels. This gives them time to fully break down food without the brain feeling starved of its glucose intake. This makes them less prone to suffer from food cravings or unnecessary hunger pangs that eventually lead to weight gain.

Having stable blood sugar level prevents negative health effects such as: blurry vision, chronic exhaustion, dry mouth, inability to concentrate/focus, irritability, unwanted food cravings, and wounds that don't heal, or heal too slowly.

5. A vegan diet helps lower the risk and/or lessen symptoms of 2 types of arthritis.

Consuming dairy, or to be more specific: consuming animal foods that are high in calcium has always been associated with ***rheumatoid arthritis*** – an inflammatory progressive condition that affects bones, ligaments and tendons. In advanced cases, this becomes physically crippling as it fuses cartilage and joints together. When this happens, bodily movement is severely limited, joints become deformed, and the person suffers from chronic pain in said afflicted area.

Another form of arthritis cause progressive bone loss and reduction of cartilage tissues. This causes bones, muscles and nerves to rub raw against each other, causing chronic inflammation in said area(s,) and subjecting it to irreversible damage. This is called **osteoarthritis**, and this condition alone increases the person's susceptibility to bacterial, fungal and viral infections.

Unfortunately, both these conditions affect more women than men, and are much more prevalent in women who are overweight and obese.

Simply consuming less meat and more fresh greens helps lessen inflammation of the joints. But by subscribing to a vegan diet, the progression of osteoarthritis slows down considerably. This lessens pain frequency and intensity of rheumatoid arthritis too. A little weight loss also helps keep stress off afflicted areas, which can aid pain management.

6. A vegan diet is a valuable tool in weight loss management.

Consuming food with intact plant fibers take longer to digest. This allows the body to produce enough insulin that can effectively break these down into glucose. This alone prevents unwanted food cravings and hunger pangs, which often lead to uncontrollable weight gain.

At the same time, most of the fresh fruits and vegetables contain little to no bad fat and cholesterol. When properly prepared, a person can consume more of these without packing on the pounds, or negatively affecting blood pressure.

A Few Things to Remember Before Starting a Vegan Diet

When following this diet, it is essential to know which products are **100% vegan-safe** or simply **vegan** (purely based on fresh or dried whole produce) or at least, **vegan-friendly** (mostly processed food, which contains grains and vegetables as primary ingredient but may also contain overly processed starches, preservatives, and salt.)

Best examples of 100% vegan-safe products are:

- Beans, fresh or dried

- Fruits, fresh or frozen

- Mushrooms, fresh or dried

- Nuts, dried, raw or lightly cooked

- Seeds, fresh, dried, or lightly cooked

- Vegetables, always fresh

    - Frozen peas are acceptable as these undergo the least amount of chemical processing, and retain most of their nutrient value.

    - Homemade pickles are also acceptable, especially if all ingredients used are 100% vegan too, including ingredients for pickling solution.

- Whole grains, fresh, or dried, lightly cooked

Some examples of vegan-friendly products are, (use these sparingly):

- Bottled or canned fruits, contains salt and high amounts of sugar, especially those pickled in syrups. Some products contain food additives like artificial food color and preservatives to improve their color and prolong their shelf lives. The longer these are steeped in syrup, the less "whole" and organic nutrients these retain.

- Bottle or canned vegetables, contains inordinate amounts of industrial-grade preservatives. Some products are artificially colored for better presentation. Others contain high amounts of salt. Both of which can cause multiple health issues.

- Bottled or canned mushrooms, contains salt (usually undeclared in product labels) and inordinate amounts of industrial-grade preservatives.

- Oils, preferably those that underwent least amount of chemical processing, like nut/seed based oils (e.g. from apple seed, beech nut, cashew, cocoa butter from cocoa beans, flaxseed/linseed, hazelnut, macadamia, pecan, pili nut, pine nut, pistachio, and walnut) and vegetable/fruit based oils (e.g. from avocado, coconut, and olives.)

Avoid any oil-based product that are hydrogenated or partially hydrogenated as these contain high amounts of trans-fat, and are usually processed with industrial strength bleach (hexane solvents.) The same goes for overly processed oils. Though these all vegetable-based, consuming these can lead to weight gain, and numerous cardiovascular diseases, despite all of their "healthy" claims.

These include oil from: corn, cottonseed, peanut, grape seed, quinoa, rapeseed (canola,) rice bran, safflower, sesame, soy bean, and sunflower.

- Soy-based products. You can cook fresh soy beans and fresh *edamame* (immature beans,) and add these safely to your vegan meal plan. But other soy-based products should be consumed sparingly.

Although technically plant-based, many of these underwent extensive chemical processing. The most abundant soy-based products in the market are manufactured on an industrial scale. This means performing routine short-cuts to boost production and keep costs down (e.g. using hexane solvents to speed up fermentation.) This also means stripping away most organic nutrients from soy beans that make these healthy in the first place.

Flavored tofu is the worst. This often contains high amounts of salt, and trace amounts of dairy, pork (bacon grease,) and seafood (anchovies.)

If you like soy-based products, it is best to use fresh beans, process the beans yourself, or buy from small-scale farmers/producers who make these the traditional way (no solvents, no added artificial flavors.) If you have to buy them at a grocery store, always check product labels before buying.

If you're a vegan, you'll want to avoid what is known as *commercial gelatin*. This substance is extracted from leftovers of meat production. Anything unusable (bones, ligaments, skins, etc.) are boiled down to extract collagen, which is its main ingredient. This is used as food extender for canned and/or pre-mixed meat, and as a preservative for bottled or canned fruits.

Somewhat disturbingly, animal-based gelatin is applied on top of commercially manufactured baked goods to make these look glossy under the light, and is a main component in cake mixes, candies, jellies, mousses, *panna cotta,* and syrups.

This is also used as thickening agent for ready-made or easy-to-make gravies and sauces. Almost all commercially-made confections like: custard filled cakes, marshmallows, and sweet flavored nuts are made with, or soaked in animal-based gelatin.

Basically, you should avoid commercially manufactured products that wiggle, jiggle, thicken, and looks shiny under the light. To be safe, check product labels. If it says "gelatin" or "halal gelatin," then it's animal-based.

If you like gelatin, look for seaweed-based alternatives. These are 100% vegan, and undergo very little chemical processing. These include:

- Agar - also called agar-agar and comes in flaked or powdered form. This has a firm set.

- Carrageenan - also called Irish moss. This can be bought in dried/desiccated moss form or in powdered form. This has a soft set.

- There is also a product called "vegan jel" which is made from "vegetable gum." This is a blanket term for overly processed vegetables, treated with artificial chemical compounds. Avoid this or use sparingly in the interest of good health.

<u>Note</u>:

There are quite a few miniscule animal by-products hidden in some food items which are otherwise 100% made from plants. While it is wise to read the details of what you put into your body, remember: Don't drive yourself crazy while sweating the small stuff.

As the *Vegan Society*'s definition states:

*"Veganism is a way of living which seeks to exclude, as far as is **possible** and **practicable**, all forms of exploitation of, and cruelty to, animals for food, clothing or any other purpose."*

Now, on to the recipes!

Conversion Chart

Imperial to Metric Volume Conversions

1/4 tsp.	=	1 ml.
1/2 tsp.	=	3 ml.
1 tsp.	=	6 ml.
1 tsp.	=	6 ml.
1 tbsp.	=	18 ml.
1/4 cup	=	59 ml.
1/3 cup	=	78 ml.
1/2 cup	=	118 ml.
2/3 cup	=	158 ml.
3/4 cup	=	177 ml.
1 cup	=	237 ml.

Imperial to Metric Weight Conversion

1 ounce	=	28 grams
2 ounces	=	55 grams
3 ounces	=	85 grams
4 ounces	=	115 grams
8 ounces	=	225 grams

Liquid Measurement Conversion

1/2 fl. oz.	=	15 ml.
1 fl. oz.	=	30 ml.
2 fl. oz.	=	59 ml.
4 fl. oz.	=	118 ml.
8 fl. oz.	=	237 ml.

Chapter 1: Beverages

Chilled or Cold Drinks

Water Infusions

Apples and Carrots in Cinnamon Water

Makes 4 servings, recommended serving size is 1 cup.

Ingredients:

4 cups of filtered water

1 cup of ice cubes

1 large red apple, cored, sliced into small wedges

1 large green apple, cored, sliced into small wedges

1 medium carrot, peeled, sliced into thin half-moons

1 medium lemon, sliced into small wedges, pips removed

1 small cinnamon bark, whole

1 tsp. of green stevia, optional

Directions:

1. - Place all ingredients into large glass pitcher.

2. - Bruise apples and lemons lightly using a wooden spoon. Stir.

3. - Chill in fridge for at least 2 hours prior to serving. Remove cinnamon stick prior to serving. (Reuse for other infusions.)

4. - Pour into tall glasses to serve. Serve immediately.

Blueberry and Citrus Infusion

Makes 4 servings, recommended serving size is 1 cup.

Ingredients:

4 cups of filtered water

1 cup of ice cubes

½ cup of fresh blueberries, rinsed well

1 large lemon, sliced into small wedges, pips removed

½ small grapefruit, sliced into small wedges, pips removed

Tall pieces of celery stalks, for garnish, optional

Directions:

1. - Except for garnish, place all ingredients into large glass pitcher.

2. - Bruise fruits lightly using a wooden spoon. Stir.

3. - Chill in fridge for at least 2 hours prior to serving.

4. - Pour into tall glasses to serve. Garnish with 1 celery stalk as stirrer, if using. Serve immediately.

Citrusy Basil and Strawberry Infusion

Makes 4 servings, recommended serving size is 1 cup.

Ingredients:

4 cups of filtered water

1 cup of ice cubes

4 large fresh strawberries, hulled, quartered

1 large key lime, sliced into small wedges, pips removed

1 medium sweet orange, sliced into small wedges, pips removed

1 handful of fresh basil leaves, whole, rinsed well, leave a few smaller leaves for garnish

Directions:

1. - Except for garnish, place all ingredients into large glass pitcher.

2. - Bruise basil leaves and strawberries lightly using a wooden spoon. Stir.

3. - Chill in fridge for at least 2 hours prior to serving.

4. - Pour into tall glasses to serve. Garnish with 1 fresh basil leaf on top. Serve immediately.

Ginger and Mango in Citrus Infusion

Makes 4 servings, recommended serving size is 1 cup.

Ingredients:

4 cups of filtered water

1 cup of ice cubes

1 cup of heaping ripe cantaloupe, peeled, cubed

1 thumb-sized fresh ginger, crushed with flat side of knife

1 large lime, sliced into small wedges, pips removed

1 large ripe mango, peeled, stone removed, cubed

1 medium tangerine, peeled, segments separated, remove membranes and visible pips, if any

Directions:

1. - Place all ingredients into large glass pitcher.
2. - Bruise fruits and ginger lightly using a wooden spoon. Stir.
3. - Chill in fridge for at least 2 hours prior to serving.

Pour into tall glasses to serve. Serve immediately.

Shaved Fruits and Vegetables Infusion

Makes 4 servings, recommended serving size is 1 cup.

Ingredients:

4 cups of filtered water

1 cup of ice cubes

1 large carrot, peeled, shaved into flat, thin ribbons using a mandolin or *spiralizer*

1 large cucumber, ends removed, deseeded, shaved into flat, thin ribbons

1 large unripe/green mango, peeled, flesh shaved into flat, thin ribbons, stone discarded

1 large zucchini, ends removed, flesh shaved into flat, thin ribbons, do not include seeds

Directions:

1. - Place all ingredients into large glass pitcher.

2. - Bruise fruits and vegetables lightly using a wooden spoon. Stir.

3. - Chill in fridge for at least 2 hours prior to serving.

4. - Pour into tall glasses to serve. Serve immediately.

Red Fruits Infusion

Makes 4 servings, recommended serving size is 1 cup.

Ingredients:

4 cups of filtered water

2 cups of heaping red watermelon, peeled, deseeded, cubed

1 cup of ice cubes

1 large blood orange, sliced into small wedges, pips removed

½ small grapefruit, sliced into small wedges, pips removed

Pomegranate seeds, for garnish, optional

Directions:

1. - Except for garnish, place all ingredients into large glass pitcher.

2. - Bruise fruits lightly using a wooden spoon. Stir.

3. - Chill in fridge for at least 2 hours prior to serving.

4. - Pour into tall glasses to serve. Garnish with a sprinkling of pomegranate seeds on top, if using. Serve immediately.

Power Juices

The following recipes entail the use of a power/slow juicer. You can also use the common blender, but in that case you should peel, discard tough parts, and roughly chop ingredients first before processing.

Apple-Pineapple Juice

Makes 1 serving.

Ingredients:

1 large apple

1 small pineapple, (use the smallest piece you can find,) top removed

1 small stalk of fresh celery, for garnish, optional

Directions:

1. - Place all ingredients into juicer. Process.

2. - Pour into tall glass. Add celery stalk for stirrer, if using. Stir. Serve immediately.

Berries Power Juice

Makes 1 serving.

Ingredients:

1 large pear

¼ cup of frozen cranberries

¼ cup of frozen blueberries

¼ cup of frozen strawberries

1 sprig of small fresh mint, for garnish, optional

Directions:

1. - Place all ingredients into juicer. Process.

2. - Pour into tall glass. Garnish with mint on top, if using. Serve immediately.

Carrot Power Juice

Makes 1 serving.

Ingredients:

1 small carrot, top removed

1 small red apple

1 small pear

1 small sprig of fresh mint, for garnish, optional

Directions:

1. - Place all ingredients into juicer. Process.

2. - Pour into tall glass. Garnish with mint on top, if using. Serve immediately.

Pineapple and Papaya Power Juice

Makes 1 serving.

Ingredients:

1 small ripe papaya, (find smallest one you can find,) quartered lengthwise, deseeded

½ small pineapple, (use smallest one you can find,) top removed, quartered lengthwise

½ cup of loosely packed fresh kale leaves, remove tough stems

½ cup of loosely packed fresh baby spinach leaves

Directions:

1. - Place all ingredients into juicer. Process.
2. - Pour into tall glass. Stir. Serve immediately.

Orange Colored Power Juice

Makes 1 serving.

Ingredients:

1 small mango, flesh scooped out

1 small carrot, tops removed

1 small ripe papaya, (use smallest one you can find,) peeled, deseeded

1 small ripe tomato

Directions:

1. - Place all ingredients into juicer. Process.

2. - Pour into tall glass. Stir. Serve immediately.

Pineapple with Greens Power Juice

Makes 1 serving.

Ingredients:

4 large kale leaves, tough stems removed, roughly torn

2 small celery stalks, remove stringy bits

½ small pineapple (use the smallest one you can find,) top removed, quartered lengthwise

½ small lime

1 generous handful of watercress

Directions:

1. - Place all ingredients into juicer. Process.

2. - Pour into tall glass. Stir. Serve immediately.

Tomato and Vegetable Power Juice

Makes 1 serving.

Ingredients:

2 large ripe tomatoes

1 small cucumber

1 small lime

1 small pear

Directions:

1. - Place all ingredients into juicer. Process.

2. - Pour into tall glass. Stir. Serve immediately.

Shakes and Smoothies

These recipes entail the use of a blender or food processor.

ABC (Almond Milk, Berries, and Cashew Nuts) Shake

Makes 2 servings.

Ingredients:

4 frozen strawberries

1 cup almond milk

1 cup frozen blueberries, reserve a couple of berries, for garnish

1 cup shaved ice or ice cubes

½ cup cashew nuts, freshly toasted on dry pan, unseasoned

1 tsp. green *stevia*, optional

Directions:

1. - Except for garnish, place all ingredients into blender and process until smooth.

2. - Pour into tall glasses to serve. Garnish with a few berries on top. Serve immediately.

Apple Pie Shake

Makes 2 servings.

Ingredients:

2 large red apples, cored, roughly chopped

1 cup almond or cashew milk

1 cup shaved ice or ice cubes

½ cup cashew nuts, freshly toasted on dry pan, unseasoned

⅛ tsp. cinnamon powder

⅛ tsp. nutmeg powder

1 pinch of ginger powder

1 tsp. green *stevia*, optional

1 tsp. raisins, for garnish, optional

Directions:

1. - Except for garnish, place all ingredients into blender and process until smooth.

2. - Pour into tall glasses to serve. Garnish each with a pinch of raisins. Serve immediately.

Blueberry, Strawberry and Flaxseed Shake

Makes 2 servings.

Ingredients:

2 large frozen bananas, overripe

2 cups almond or coconut milk

1 cup shaved ice or ice cubes

1 cup, heaping frozen strawberries, halved

1½ Tbsp. flaxseed, freshly toasted on dry pan, unseasoned

1 Tbsp. green *stevia*

Directions:

1. - Except for garnish, place all ingredients into blender and process until smooth.

2. - Pour into tall glasses to serve. Serve immediately.

Chocolate Banana Shake

Makes 2 servings.

Ingredients:

2 large frozen bananas, overripe, peeled, roughly chopped

1 cup heaping shaved ice or ice cubes

1 cup almond or rice milk

6 Tbsp. heaping cocoa powder or breakfast cocoa

1 tsp. almond slivers, freshly toasted on dry pan, unseasoned, for garnish, optional

Directions:

1. - Except for garnish, place all ingredients into blender and process until smooth.

2. - Pour into tall glasses to serve. Sprinkle with almond slivers. Serve immediately.

Coconut Salad Shake

Makes 2 servings.

Ingredients:

1 large ripe mango, peeled, flesh scooped

1 can, 15 oz. coconut cream

1 cup, heaping shaved ice or ice cubes

1 cup coconut milk

½ tsp. pumpkin seeds, freshly toasted on dry pan, unseasoned

1 large passion fruit, seeds scooped out, divided into 2 equal portions, for garnish, optional

Directions:

1. - Except for garnish, place all ingredients into blender and process until smooth.

2. - Pour into tall glasses to serve. Spoon equal portions of passion fruits seeds on top, if using. Serve immediately.

Dill and Cucumber Smoothie

Makes 2 servings.

Ingredients:

5 large sprigs of dill fronds, rinsed, drained, reserve a few for garnish

1 large cucumber, ends removed, deseeded

1 large lime, freshly squeezed, remove pips

1½ cup shaved ice or ice cubes

¼ cup shelled pistachios, lightly toasted on dry pan, unseasoned

Directions:

1. - Except for garnish, place all ingredients into blender and process until smooth.

2. - Pour into tall glasses to serve. Sprinkle a few pieces of dill fronds on top. Serve immediately.

Fruity Green Smoothie

Makes 2 ½ cups of smoothie.

Ingredients:

1 cup water

1 cup kale

1 cup baby spinach

1 medium apple, cored and chopped

1 medium orange, peeled and separated

½ large banana, frozen

Directions:

1. - Put every ingredient into a high-velocity blender.

2. - Blend on a high setting for 3-5 minutes, or until it acquires a smooth consistency. Serve.

Tip: Keep any leftovers refrigerated in an airtight container.

Walnut Smoothie

Makes 2 servings.

Ingredients:

2 large dried dates, pitted, halved

2 large frozen overripe bananas, peeled, roughly chopped

1 cup shaved ice or ice cubes

½ cup, loosely packed shelled walnuts, freshly roasted on dry pan, unseasoned, reserve 2 halves for garnish

½ cup coconut water, unsweetened

1 tsp. lemon juice, freshly squeezed

Directions:

1. - Except for garnish, place all ingredients into blender and process until smooth.

2. - Pour into tall glasses to serve. Add walnut halves on top. Serve immediately.

Hot or Warm Drinks

Herbal Infusions (Caffeine-Free)

Apples and Chamomile Herbal Infusion

Makes 4 servings, recommended serving size is 1 cup.

Ingredients:

4 cups filtered water, freshly boiled to 212°F or 100°C

¼ cup, loosely packed chamomile flowers (tea-grade,) rinsed well, drained, approximately 2 mini teabags

1 small green apple, cored, halved, sliced into thick half-moons

1 2-inch long dried cinnamon bark

Directions:

1. - Pour all ingredients into coffee or tea press (or any heat-safe container.)

2. - Steep herbal infusion for 5 to 8 minutes. Strain. Serve immediately.

Berry and Lemon Herbal Infusion

Makes 4 servings, recommended serving size is 1 cup.

Ingredients:

4 cups filtered water, freshly boiled to 212°F or 100°C

¼ cup fresh blueberries, rinsed, drained

¼ cup fresh blackberries, rinsed, drained

¼ cup fresh raspberries, rinsed, drained

¼ cup, loosely packed lemon balm leaves (tea-grade,) rinsed well, drained, approximately 2 mini teabags

Directions:

1. - Pour all ingredients into coffee or tea press (or any heat-safe container.)

2. - Steep herbal infusion for 5 to 8 minutes. Strain. Serve immediately.

Citrus and Peppermint Herbal Infusion

Makes 4 servings, recommended serving size is 1 cup.

Ingredients:

4 cups filtered water, freshly boiled to 212°F or 100°C

1 cup, heaping red grapes, preferably seedless

¼ cup, loosely packed peppermint leaves (tea grade,) rinsed well, drained, approximately 2 mini teabags

1 small blood orange, halved, sliced into thick half-moons, pips removed

1 small sweet orange, halved, sliced into thick half-moons, pips removed

Directions:

1. - Pour all ingredients into coffee or tea press (or any heat-safe container.)

2. - Steep herbal infusion for 5 to 8 minutes. Strain. Serve immediately.

Forest Leaves Herbal Infusion

Makes 4 servings, recommended serving size is 1 cup.

Ingredients:

4 cups filtered water, freshly boiled to 212°F or 100°C

⅛ cup, loosely packed dried blackberry leaves (tea grade,) rinsed once with boiling water, drained, approx. 1 mini teabag

⅛ cup, loosely packed dried lemon balm leaves (tea grade,) rinsed once with boiling water, drained, approx. 1 mini teabag

⅛ cup, loosely packed dried hawthorn leaves (tea grade,) rinsed once with boiling water, drained, approx. 1 mini teabag

⅛ tsp., per cup green *stevia*, optional

Directions:

1. - Pour all ingredients into coffee or tea press (or any heat-safe container.)

2. - Steep herbal infusion for 5 to 8 minutes. Strain. Serve infusion in cups. Stir in green *stevia*, if desired. Serve immediately.

Fruity Ginger Herbal Infusion

Makes 4 servings, recommended serving size is 1 cup.

Ingredients:

4 cups filtered water, freshly boiled to 212°F or 100°C

½ cup, heaping fresh raspberries, or any berries of choice

½ cup fresh pomegranate seeds

2 large cardamom pods, lightly crushed

1 thumb-sized ginger, peeled, lightly crushed

1 small lemon, halved, sliced into thick half-moons, visible pips removed

⅛ tsp., per cup green *stevia,* optional

Directions:

1. - Pour all ingredients into coffee or tea press (or any heat-safe container).

2. - Steep herbal infusion for 5 to 8 minutes. Strain. Serve infusion in cups. Stir in green *stevia*, if desired. Serve immediately.

Lavender and Mint Herbal Infusion

Makes 4 servings, recommended serving size is 1 cup.

Ingredients:

4 cups filtered water, freshly boiled to 212°F or 100°C

½ cup, loosely packed dried peppermint leaves (tea grade,) rinsed once with hot water, drained

¼ cup, loosely packed dried lavender (tea grade,) rinsed once with hot water, drained

1 small apple, cored, halved, sliced into thick half-moons

⅛ tsp., per cup green *stevia*, optional

Directions:

1. - Except for green *stevia*, pour all ingredients into coffee or tea press (or any heat-safe container).

2. - Steep herbal infusion for 5 to 8 minutes. Strain. Serve infusion in cups. Stir in green *stevia*, if desired. Serve immediately.

Raspberry Herbal Infusion

Makes 4 servings, recommended serving size is 1 cup.

Ingredients:

4 cups filtered water, freshly boiled to 212°F or 100°C

½ cup, loosely packed and dried raspberry leaves (tea grade,) rinsed once with hot water, drained

½ cup, heaping fresh raspberries, rinsed

1 small lemon, halved, sliced into thick half-moons, visible pips removed

⅛ tsp., per cup green *stevia,* optional

Directions:

1. - Except for green *stevia,* pour all ingredients into coffee or tea press (or any heat-safe container).

2. - Steep herbal infusion for 5 to 8 minutes. Strain. Serve infusion in cups. Stir in green *stevia,* if desired. Serve immediately.

Chapter 2: Sweets

No-Bake Sweets

Chocolate Chip Granola Bars

Makes around 10 bars.

Ingredients:

2 cups rolled oats

½ cup oat bran

½ cup sunflower seed butter (can be substituted with peanut butter)

½ cup coconut oil

½ cup brown rice syrup (can be substituted with corn syrup)

¼ cup sunflower seeds (can be substituted with pine nuts or pumpkin seeds)

¼ cup shredded coconut (can be substituted with shredded almonds)

Dark chocolate chips, as desired

Directions:

1. - Prepare a baking tray (with edges) with bakery paper.

2. - Combine the rolled oats, oat bran, shredded coconut and sunflower seeds in a large bowl. Mix well.

3. - Combine the sunflower seed butter, brown rice syrup and coconut oil in a bowl which is safe for microwaving. Microwave the mixture for 1.5 to 2 minutes, or until it melts.

4. - Pour the liquid mixture into the bowl with the dry mixture. Blend well.

5. - Put the combined mixture into the baking tray and press it with your hands until the top is somewhat flat. Spread as much dark chocolate chips on top as you like.

6. - Put it in the refrigerator for 2-3 hours.

7. - Remove the hardened mixture from the tray and cut it into evenly sized bars. Serve.

Tip: Keep any leftovers refrigerated.

Chewy "Walmond" Bars

Makes around 10 bars.

Ingredients:

Dry ingredients

¼ cup walnuts

¼ cup almonds

½ cup unsweetened coconut flakes

1/3 cup hemp seeds

¼ cup dates, pitted and chopped, about 5 whole dates or so

¼ cup dark chocolate chips

Wet ingredients

1/3 cup maple syrup

2 Tbsp. coconut oil

½ Tbsp. grated ginger

1 tsp. vanilla

Mix-in

½ cup almond flour

2 scoops hemp protein powder (can be substituted with other vegan protein powder such as sprouted rice or soy)

3 Tbsp. raw cacao powder

3 Tbsp. Chia seeds

2 Tbsp. Maca powder

1 Tbsp., heaping, frozen raspberries, optional

Directions:

1. - Combine all of the dry ingredients in a food processor and blend carefully until everything is mixed up. There should be small chunks of nuts and fruits left. Pour the dry mix into a bowl.

2. - Pour the wet ingredients into the food processor or a blender, and mix it up until it is properly combined.

3. - Pour the wet blend onto the dry blend and mix them up.

4. - Then, incorporate all the "Mix-ins" to the dry and wet blend until it is combined.

5. - Spread the final mixture evenly with preferred thickness into a baking pan or a similar container, and then place it in the fridge. After a few hours, the texture will become somewhat hard and chewy.

6. - Once it has hardened, cut it into desired shapes. Serve.

Tip: Store any leftovers in an air tight container in the fridge.

Sweet Banana Nut Bars

Makes around 4 bars.

Ingredients:

½ cup mashed banana

¼ cup raw, cut up almonds, can be replaced by another nut of your choice

2 scoops vanilla flavored vegan protein, any kind

2 Tbsp. coconut flour

1 Tbsp. water

1 tsp. vanilla extract

½ tsp. cinnamon

1 tsp. stevia, or another sweetener of your choice (optional)

Directions:

1. - Place all the ingredients in a bowl and mix them together until the texture is smooth.

2. - Roll the mixture evenly out on baking tray covered with bakery paper.

3. - Refrigerate it for about 1 - 2 hours.

4. - When it has sufficiently hardened, cut it into 4 pieces. Serve.

Tip: Keep any leftovers refrigerated.

Banana and Berry Sweetened Oats with Coconut Milk

Makes 4 servings, recommended serving size is 1 cup.

Ingredients:

For oats

1½ cups water

½ cup steel cut oats (do not use instant or quick cooking oats)

1 pinch kosher salt

½ cup coconut milk (can be substituted with rice milk or any other vegan milk of choice)

For fruits

1 medium banana, preferably overripe, mashed

½ cup frozen blueberries

½ cup frozen strawberries, quartered

1 Tbsp., heaping, frozen blackberries, optional

1 Tbsp., heaping, frozen raspberries, optional

Directions:

1. - <u>To prepare oats</u>: except for coconut milk, place all ingredients into pot set over medium heat. Let this come to a boil, stirring often.

2. - Turn down heat to lowest setting. Put lid partially on. Simmer for 5 to 10 minutes, depending on how chewy you want your oats to be. Turn off heat.

3. - <u>For the seasoning</u>: add in fruits. Stir. Secure lid of pot. Let oats rest for 3 to 5 minutes. Add in coconut milk. Stir. Ladle into single serve bowls. Serve.

Boiled Plantains

Makes 4 servings, recommended serving size is 1 large plantain per person.

Ingredients:

4 large plantains, preferably overripe and slightly mushy

Water, just enough for boiling

Directions:

1. - Place plantains in deep saucepan set over high heat. Pour just enough water to completely submerge fruits. Let water come to a boil.

2. - Put lid on. Turn down heat to lowest setting. Cook plantains until water changes color, about 15 minutes.

3. - Turn off heat. Remove plantains and discard cooking water.

4. - Let plantains cool slightly before peeling/serving.

Note: You can serve boiled plantains warm, at room temperature, or chilled. Peel only prior to eating.

Brownies in Mugs

Makes 4 servings.

Ingredients:

½ cup all-purpose flour

½ cup rice milk

6 Tbsp. *muscovado* or palm sugar, crumbled

4 Tbsp. unsweetened cocoa powder or breakfast cocoa

4 Tbsp. coconut oil

2 Tbsp. coconut milk (substitute water, if unavailable)

½ tsp. baking powder

¼ tsp. kosher salt

For garnish, both optional

4 Tbsp. hazelnut chocolate spread, vegan-safe

2 large cashew nuts, lightly roasted, unseasoned, halved

Directions:

1. - Place all ingredients in large mixing bowl. Whisk well until lumps disappear. Divide batter into 4 equal portions.

2. - Pour each portion into large mugs, approximately 14 oz. each or larger. Make sure there is enough room for the cake to rise in.

3. - Place each mug in the microwave oven. Cook each cake for 1 minute and 10 seconds on highest setting, or until cake crests the mug rims. (Cooking time may depend on power settings for microwave ovens, so keep an eye on the cakes to prevent burning.) Carefully remove cake from microwave oven. Repeat step for other mug cakes. Cool slightly for easier handling.

4. - To assemble: place a level tablespoon of hazelnut chocolate spread in the center of each mug cake, if using. Top off with 1 cashew nut half, if using. Serve.

Coconut and Jackfruit Flapjacks

Makes 2 servings, or 8 small pancakes.

Recommended serving size is 1 stack of 4 pancakes.

Ingredients:

Coconut oil, for pan frying

Dry ingredients:

1¼ cup whole wheat flour

½ cup shredded, desiccated coconut

1 tsp. baking powder

¼ tsp. baking soda

¼ tsp. all spice powder

¼ tsp. cinnamon powder

¼ tsp. nutmeg powder

1 pinch, small kosher salt

Wet ingredients:

¾ cup coconut milk

¾ cup coconut water, (substitute plain water)

½ tsp. vanilla extract

Toppings:

½ cup fresh coconut flesh, shredded, divided

¼ cup sweet jackfruit or *langka*, used bottled jackfruit in light syrup, drained lightly, divided (substitute fresh mangoes, if unavailable)

Directions:

1. - Pour small amount of coconut oil into non-stick frying pan set over medium heat. Swirl oil around to lightly grease cooking surface.

2. - Pour all dry ingredients into mixing bowl. Stir. Make well in the center.

3. - Pour in coconut milk, coconut water, and vanilla extract in the center. Whisk until there are no more lumps in the batter.

4. - Add in half portions of fresh coconut and jackfruit. Stir.

5. - Pour ¼ cup of batter into prepared frying pan. Cook until edges are set and center is no longer runny. Flip. Cook other side for 1 minute. Transfer to a plate. Repeat step to cook remaining batter.

6. - To assemble: stack 4 pieces of pancakes. Top off with fresh shredded coconut and few pieces of jackfruit. Repeat step for other pancake stack. Serve immediately.

Elvis' Tricked Out Grilled Peanut Butter Sandwich

Makes 2 servings, or 1 large sandwich, recommended serving is ½ sandwich.

Ingredients:

2 slices extra thick-cut vegan rye bread, or any vegan-safe wholegrain bread, toasted lightly on both sides

Coconut oil, for pan frying

½ tsp. confectioner's or powdered sugar, vegan-safe, for garnish, optional

¼ tsp. crushed almonds, freshly toasted on dry pan, unseasoned, for garnish, optional

For filling:

1 large banana, just overripe, sliced into ¼ inch-thick disks

¼ cup fresh blueberries, or any fresh berries of choice, reserve some for garnish, later on

1 Tbsp., heaping, peanut butter, smooth

1 Tbsp., heaping, coconut butter, preferably homemade (recipe can be found at the start of the *Baked Sweets* section)

Directions:

1. - <u>To prepare sandwich</u>: spread peanut butter on 1 slice of rye bread, and coconut butter on the other.

2. - Layer in sliced bananas and fresh blueberries on top of peanut butter. Seal sandwich with other slice of rye bread.

3. - <u>To cook</u>: lightly grease non-stick frying pan with coconut oil. Set pan over medium heat.

4. - Grill sandwich until well toasted on both side, about 2 to 3 minutes on both sides. Transfer to a plate to cool slightly before slicing in half diagonally.

5. - <u>To serve</u>: place half sandwich on a plate. Sprinkle half portion of almonds and powdered sugar on top, if using. Serve immediately. This is best served with chilled, unsweetened almond milk.

Plantain Meal with Tropical Fruits Salad

Makes 4 servings, recommended serving size is 1 cup.

Ingredients:

4 large *Boiled Plantains* (recipe included earlier in this section)

For toppings:

2 tsp., heaping, desiccated coconut, lightly toasted on dry pan, divided, optional

2 tsp., heaping, cashew or shelled walnuts, freshly toasted on dry pan, roughly crushed, divided, optional

1 large, ripe mango, peeled, stone removed, diced, divided

1 medium, ripe papaya, peeled, deseeded, diced, divided

1 splash of coconut or almond milk, optional

Directions:

1. - To prepare plantain meal: peel boiled plantains. Roughly mash for added texture.

2. - Divide into 4 equal portions and ladle into individual bowls. Microwave on highest setting for 3 to 5 seconds to warm through, if desired.

3. - <u>To assemble</u>: add equal portions of diced mango and papaya on top of plantain meal. Sprinkle equal portions of toasted desiccated coconut and cashew nuts, if using. Stir. Add splash of coconut milk, if desired. Serve immediately.

Note: substitute seasonal berries and fruits of choice.

Spiced Poached Pears in White Wine

Makes 4 servings, recommended serving size is 1 pear.

Ingredients:

5 dried cloves, optional

4 medium ripe pears, skins scrubbed well, lightly pricked with a fork

1 cinnamon stick, 2-inches long

1 small lime, zest removed using vegetable peeler, juiced

1 small star anise, optional

1 small vanilla pod, sliced lengthwise, insides scraped

1 cup white wine

½ cup palm sugar, crumbled

Water, for boiling

Directions:

1. - Place all ingredients in deep saucepan set over high heat. Pour just enough water to completely submerge fruits. Let water come to a boil, uncovered.

2. - Turn down heat to medium heat setting. Continue cooking until pears are fork tender, and cooking liquid is reduced in half, about 25 to 30 minutes.

3. - Turn off heat. Remove cooked pears to a plate.

4. - Strain out and discard solids from cooking liquid. Set saucepan over high heat again. Reduce liquid some more until this looks syrupy. Turn off heat. Cool to room temperature.

5. - To serve: place cooked pears into individual ramekins or bowls.

6. - Spoon about 1 tablespoon (or more) of the reduced liquid on top. Serve.

Strawberry Flax Seed Jam

Makes 2 cups of jam.

Ingredients:

2 cups destemmed strawberries

2 Tbsp. flax seeds

2 tsp. brown sugar (optional)

Water, as required

Directions:

1. - Chop the strawberries into smaller pieces.

2. - Place the chopped strawberries, flax seeds and brown sugar (optional, if you want it sweeter) into a blender. Blend on medium speed. Carefully add water until it reaches the desired consistency.

3. - Pour the mixture into a saucepan and heat on medium temperature until the jam begins to bubble. Reduce the heat and simmer for around 5 minutes, or until the jam thickens in consistency.

4. - Pour the jam into a glass container. Put it in the refrigerator until it cools down. Serve.

Tip: Goes great with the Easy Fluffy Vegan Rolls in the Baked Savory Snacks section.

Baked Sweets

Homemade Coconut Butter on Homemade Vegan Rye Bread

Makes about ½ cup coconut butter and 1 rye bread loaf.

Recommended serving size: 1 thick slice of bread and 1 tsp. level of coconut butter.

Ingredients:

For coconut butter:

1 package, 7 oz. coconut flakes, high quality

For Rye Bread:

Olive oil, for greasing

Wet ingredients:

¼ tsp. active dry yeast, approx. ¼ ounce package

2 cups warm water

1 Tbsp. pure maple syrup

Dry ingredients:

2 cups bread flour, add more later for kneading

1½ cups dark rye flour, finely milled

½ cup dark rye flour, coarsely milled

1 Tbsp. palm sugar, crumbled 3 tsp. black caraway seeds, lightly toasted on dry pan (no oil,) reserve 1 tsp. for topping

1¾ tsp. kosher salt

Directions:

1. - <u>To make coconut butter</u>: place coconut flakes into blender. Process for 5 to 10 minutes until thick and smooth. Scrape sides down often. Transfer coconut butter into non-reactive container with lid. Rest butter for 15 minutes before using.

2. - <u>To make bread</u>: pour yeast and water in a bowl. Whisk well to combine. Set aside until mixture becomes frothy, about 10 minutes.

3. - Except for 1 teaspoon of caraway seeds, add in dry ingredients into large mixing bowl. Fork through to mix. Make a well in the center.

4. - Pour in maple syrup and yeast mixture. Mix until dough comes together.

5. - Turn out dough on lightly floured surface. Knead until dough no longer sticks to your hands, adding more bread flour as you go. Form this into a ball.

6. - Lightly grease another bowl with small amount of olive oil. Roll dough into oil. Cover with saran wrap. Let dough rise until doubled in size, about 1½ hours.

7. - Punch dough down. Form into ball again. Let this rise for another 1½ hours.

8. - Lightly grease the insides of an 8½" x 4½" x 2½' bread loaf pan with olive oil. Turn out the dough into loaf pan. Sprinkle remaining caraway seeds on top. Let bread have its final rising for 40 to 50 minutes, or until dough slightly crests the top of the loaf pan.

9. - Meanwhile, preheat oven to 375°F (190°C).

10. - Place loaf pan on middle rack of oven and bake for 40 to 45 minutes, or until top is golden brown.

11. - Remove loaf pan from oven and set on cooling rack until bread comes to room temperature.

12. - Slide out bread from loaf pan. Slice only when completely cooled.

13. - <u>To assemble</u>: lightly toast or warm through 1 rye bread slice. Spread 1 teaspoon of coconut butter on top. Serve immediately.

Raspberry Glazed Almond Cupcakes

Makes 12 small cupcakes, recommended serving size is 2 cupcakes.

Ingredients:

For glaze

1½ cup confectioner's sugar, vegan-safe

¼ cup frozen raspberries, thawed, do not drain

2 tsp. almond milk

½ tsp. lime juice, freshly squeezed

¼ tsp. vanilla extract

For cupcakes:

Dry ingredients:

1 cup almond flour, coarsely milled

1 cup almond flour, finely milled

½ cup white sugar, vegan-safe

1 tsp. baking powder

1 tsp. baking soda

¼ tsp. cinnamon powder

¼ tsp. nutmeg powder

Wet ingredients

1 cup frozen raspberries, thawed

1 cup almond milk, or any non-dairy milk substitute

½ cup applesauce, unsweetened, vegan-safe

2 Tbsp. avocado or coconut oil, at room temperature

2 Tbsp. water

1 tsp. vanilla extract

Directions:

1. - <u>To make glaze</u>: mix ingredients in a bowl. Whisk well to incorporate as much air into glaze as possible. Cover with sheet of saran wrap. Chill prior to use.

2. - <u>To make cupcakes</u>: preheat oven to 325°F/160°C. Place paper liners into cupcake tins. Set aside.

3. - Pour dry ingredients into large mixing bowl. Fork through to combine.

4. - Pour wet ingredients into large mixing bowl. Whisk until frothy. Gradually pour mixture into dry ingredients. Mixing only until combined. Don't overwork batter.

5. - Spoon into prepared cupcake tins, filling each ¾ full.

6. - Bake for 15 to 18 minutes, or until toothpick inserted in center comes out clean.

7. - Remove tin from oven, and set on cake rack to cool completely before removing individual cupcakes.

8. - Spoon small amount of glaze on top, approximately 1 teaspoon or more. Serve.

9. - To assemble: spoon ½ teaspoon (or less) of glaze on each cupcake. Serve. Keep rest in fridge.

Vegan Chocolate Cupcakes with Ginger & Orange

Makes 24 small cupcakes, recommended serving size is 2 cupcakes.

Ingredients:

For glaze:

1 cup. vegan margarine, softened at room temperature

4 cups. powdered sugar

½ cup. cocoa powder

¼ cup. soy milk

2 Tbsp. cocoa powder

1 Tbsp. vanilla

1 Tbsp. orange juice

1/8 tsp. salt

For cupcakes:

Dry ingredients

3 cups. all-purpose flour

1½ cups. Sugar

2/3 cup. unsweetened cocoa powder

2 Tbsp. freshly grated ginger

4 Tbsp. zested orange peel

1 tsp. salt

2 tsp. baking soda

2 tsp. pure vanilla extract

Wet ingredients

1 2/3 cups water

1 cup neutral oil, such as canola

4 Tbsp. cider vinegar

1 Tbsp. orange juice

Directions:

1. - To make cupcakes: preheat oven to 325°F/160°C. Place paper liners into cupcake tins. Set aside.

2. - Whisk together the flour, sugar, cocoa powder, baking soda, and salt. Add the water, oil, vanilla, orange juice, ginger, and orange peel. Stir to combine. Add the vinegar and stir quickly.

3. - The batter will become somewhat foamy and lighter in color as you incorporate the vinegar. The batter will turn darker again once the vinegar is properly mixed in.

4. - Fill the prepared cupcake tins ¾ full. Bake for about 15 - 18 minutes, or until the top of the cupcakes spring back when gently pressed with a finger.

5. - Cool in the pan for about 5 minutes. Wait until the cupcakes are cool until you apply the glaze.

6. - <u>To make frosting:</u> whip the margarine with a hand or stand mixer until it has a creamy consistency. Add the powdered sugar and cocoa powder. Gradually whip in the soy milk, then the vanilla, orange juice, and salt and blend the mixture until it is creamy and lighter in color.

7. - <u>To assemble:</u> apply ½ teaspoon of glaze on each cupcake. Serve. Keep the rest of the glaze cooled in fridge.

Twice-Baked Sweet Potatoes and Purple Yam

Makes 4 servings, recommended serving size 1 heaping cup.

Ingredients:

2 large sweet potatoes, peeled, sliced into thick matchsticks

1 large purple yam, peeled, sliced into thick matchstick, (substitute taro, if desired)

Water, for spraying

1 dash fine kosher salt

For sugar glaze:

2 Tbsp. olive oil, for drizzling

2 Tbsp. brown sugar or palm sugar, crumbled, add more for a sweeter blend

1/8 tsp. cinnamon powder

1/8 tsp. nutmeg powder

Directions:

1. - To prepare sugar glaze: except for olive oil, combine all ingredients in a small bowl. Toss well to combine.

2. - To bake potatoes: preheat oven to 350°F (175°C) for at least 10 minutes prior to use. Line a baking sheet with parchment paper.

3. - Place sweet potato and yam matchsticks on prepared baking sheet. Lay these flat on the sheet to ensure even cooking. Spray with small amount of water to steam root vegetables faster. Add a dash of salt for flavor.

4. - Bake these in hot oven for 45 minutes or until fork tender. Remove baking sheet from oven, but do not turn off heat.

5. - Drizzle oil on top of vegetables. Sprinkle prepared sugar glaze on top. Using a pair of tongs, toss to evenly coat sweet potatoes and yam.

6. - Return baking sheet into oven, and cook vegetables for another 5 to 7 minutes, or until sugar melts a little. Turn off heat.

7. - Remove baking sheet from oven and place on cooling rack. Let vegetables cool completely to room temperature before serving.

8. - <u>To serve</u>: divide sweet potatoes and taro into 4 equal portions. Plate. Serve.

Hazelnut & Olive Oil Shortbread

Makes 18 to 22 small cookie slices.

Ingredients:

1 ¼ cup. hazelnut flour

¾ cup. flour

¼ cup. brown sugar

¼ cup. powdered sugar

1 tsp. kosher salt

1 tsp. Vanilla

½ cup. extra-virgin light olive oil

1 zested lemon

For glaze:

¼ cup. powdered sugar

1 Tbsp. lemon juice, squeezed from the lemon used earlier

Directions:

1. - Heat the oven to 375°F (190°).

2. - Whisk together the hazelnut meal, flour, brown sugar, 1/4 cup powdered sugar, salt and a handful of lemon zest.

3. - Mix the vanilla and olive oil. The dough will start to appear sandy and somewhat crumbly.

4. - Press the dough firmly into a baking dish.

5. - Bake for 20 minutes or until golden brown around the edges. Immediately cut the shortbread into diamond or square shapes.

6. - Let the shortbread cool completely before lifting them out of the pan.

7. - Whisk together 1 tablespoon of the lemon's juice and 1/4 cup powdered sugar into a glaze, and drizzle it over the fresh, warm shortbread. Serve.

Peanut Butter & Jam Cookies

Makes around 30 small cookies.

Ingredients:

2 cups chickpeas

2/3 cup. strawberry jam (see recipe at the end of the *No-bake Sweets* section)

½ cup. maple syrup

½ cup. peanut butter

2 tsp. vanilla

½ tsp. baking powder

½ tsp. baking soda

¼ tsp. salt

Directions:

1. - Preheat the oven to 350°F (175°C).

2. - Excluding the strawberry jam, put all of the ingredients into a food processor.

3. - Blend on a high setting until it is thoroughly mixed, about 3 minutes.

4. - Prepare mini muffin shapes on a baking tray and spray them with cooking spray. Put around 1 Tbsp. of the muffin mix into each shape. Using a spoon, make a hole in the center of each cookie.

5. - Put one large tsp. of strawberry jam into the hole of each cookie.

6. - Bake the cookies at 350°F (175°C) for around 20 minutes, or until the edges of the cookies start to turn brown. Serve.

Chapter 3: Savory Snacks

No-Bake Savory Snacks

Citrus-Flavored Kebab

Makes 4 servings, recommended serving size is 1 kebab.

Ingredients:

For vegetables:

8 cherry tomatoes, whole

1 piece, medium onion, peeled, sliced into large wedges

1 piece, medium apple, cored, cubed

1 piece, small zucchini, ends removed, sliced into ½ inch thick medallions

½ piece, small green bell pepper, deseeded, ribbed, sliced into squares

1 can, 4 oz. button mushrooms, whole, rinsed well, drained, approximately 4 large or 8 smaller pieces

For citrus seasoning:

1 piece, medium sweet orange, freshly juiced

¼ tsp, sugar

1 pinch kosher salt

1 pinch smoked paprika powder

1 dash black pepper

Directions:

1. - Soak 4 bamboo skewers in water for at least 1 hour prior to use.

2. - <u>To make seasoning</u>: combine all ingredients in a bowl. Whisk well until salt and sugar dissolves.

3. - <u>To prepare kebabs</u>: preheat stovetop or electric grill for 5 minutes prior to use.

4. - Thread equal portions of fruits, mushrooms and vegetables on bamboo skewers.

5. - Using a pastry brush, generously season kebabs.

6. - Grill these for 7 to 10 minutes, rotating kebabs often. These are done when some tomato skins blister and almost fall away.

7. - Place kebabs on plate. Slather more seasoning, if desired. Cool slightly before serving.

Grilled Corn with Coconut Butter

Makes 4 servings, recommended serving size is ½ corn.

Ingredients:

2 large fresh sweet or Japanese corn on cob, peeled, silks and pointy tops removed, each cob halved into equal portions

2 Tbsp. coconut butter, at room temperature, add more if desired

1 sprinkling kosher salt

Directions:

1. - Soak 4 bamboo skewers in water for at least 1 hour prior to use.

2. - <u>To prepare corn</u>: preheat stovetop or electric grill for 5 minutes prior to use.

3. - Skewer 1 piece of corn on to 1 bamboo skewer. Using a pastry brush, lightly grease corn with coconut butter.

4. - Grill these for 7 to 10 minutes, rotating the corn often.

5. - Remove corn to a plate. Grease with more coconut butter, if desired.

6. - Sprinkle lightly with kosher salt. Cool slightly before serving.

Savory Veggie Fritters

Makes 4 fritters, recommended serving size is 1 piece.

Ingredients:

1 large red onion/shallot, peeled, julienned

1 large Russet potato, peeled, roughly grated

1 large sweet potato, peeled, roughly grated

1 medium carrot, top removed, roughly grated

1 small garlic, grated

1 cup, packed fresh spinach leaves, julienned

1½ Tbsp. corn or coconut flour

1 Tbsp. red pepper flakes

¼ tsp. smoky or sweet paprika

1 pinch, generous, kosher salt, add more later if desired

White pepper, to taste

Coconut or palm oil, for frying

½ small lime, sliced into 4 wedges, for garnish, optional

¼ cup chives, minced, for garnish, optional

Directions:

1. - <u>To prepare vegetables</u>: place carrot, kale leaves, onion, potato, sweet potato and salt into a large piece of cheesecloth. Toss ingredients with your fingers to mix.

2. - Bundle cheesecloth up and squeeze out as much excess moisture as possible. This will prevent fritters from spitting oil during cooking. Transfer vegetables into a large mixing bowl.

3. - Except for coconut oil and chives, add in remaining ingredients into bowl. Mix.

4. - Divide into 4 equal fritters. Roughly shape into patties.

5. - <u>To cook</u>: pour just enough cooking oil into small non-stick frying pan to lightly grease cooking surface. Set frying pan over medium heat. Wait for oil to become slightly smoky before cooking fritters.

6. - Place 1 fritter into frying pan. Fry until golden brown on first side, approximately 2 to 3 minutes. Flip. Cook the other side for another 2 minutes. Transfer cooked fritter to a plate lined with paper towel to remove excess grease. Repeat step until all fritters are cooked.

Homemade Hummus

Makes 1 ½ cup of hummus.

Ingredients:

½ lime

1 ½ cup chickpeas

¼ cup diced tomatoes

2 Tbsp. poblano pepper, finely diced

1 ½ Tbsp. water

1 Tbsp. parsley, chopped

1 tsp. Tahini

¾ tsp. salt

½ 1 tsp. sea salt

½ tsp. garlic oil

½ tsp. sesame oil

½ tsp. white sesame seeds

Directions:

1. - Except for the lime, put all of the ingredients in a food processor.

2. - Squeeze the juice from the lime over the ingredients.

3. - Blend until the consistency is smooth. Adding more water if necessary.

4. - Pour the hummus into a small bowl. Serve.

Tip: Can be served with a variety of chips and crackers found in the *Baked Savory Snacks* section.

Simple & Savory Guacamole

Makes 2 servings.

Ingredients:

1 avocado, ripe

1 small garlic clove, minced

½ lime

¼ cup diced tomatoes

2 Tbsp. poblano pepper, finely diced

½ tsp. sea salt

Directions:

1. - Cut the avocado in half, remove the large seed.

2. - With a spoon, scoop the flesh of the avocado into a small bowl.

3. - Juice the lime piece over the avocado.

4. - Mash the lime juice and the avocado together until a smooth consistency is achieved.

5. - Add the diced tomatoes, poblano pepper and garlic. Use a spoon or the back of a fork to gently knead them into the mashed avocado.

6. - Season with sea salt until satisfied.

Tip: Can be served with tortilla chips (recipe can be found in the *Baked Savory Snacks* section).

Baked Savory Snacks

Homemade Tortillas

Makes 15 servings.

Ingredients:

12 oz. cornmeal

2 cups water

2 tsp. salt

Directions:

1. - Combine the cornmeal and salt in a bowl.

2. - Add warm water.

3. - Mix the ingredients with a large spoon.

4. - Knead the mixture for 3-5 minutes until it looks doughy (if you want softer tortillas, add around 1,5 oz. of extra virgin olive oil)

5. - Shape the dough into 15 small balls.

6. - Place a large piece of bakery paper or plastic on a flat surface, and put a ball of dough on it. Place another piece of bakery paper or plastic on top of the dough, and use a pan to flatten the ball into a thin tortilla.

7. - Place each tortilla on a skillet, one at a time. Cook for about 2 minutes on each side on a medium temperature until it stops looking doughy. Serve.

Baked Tortilla Chips

Makes 2 servings.

Ingredients:

1 whole cayenne pepper

4 tortillas (see previous recipe)

½ tsp onion powder

½ tsp. garlic powder

½ tsp. nutritional yeast

¼ tsp. sweet paprika

Extra virgin olive oil, as needed

Directions:

1. - Cut the tortillas (either made from the previous recipe or store-bought) into triangle shapes and place them on a tray with bakery paper.

2. - Gently cover them with a thin layer of olive oil.

3. - Preheat your oven to 390° (200°C). Bake the tortillas for 5 minutes.

4. - Take them out of the oven and let them cool down until their consistency becomes crunchy.

5. - Put all of the spicy ingredients in a food processor and blend them together.

6. - Mix the spices with the tortilla chips (Tip: If you want the spices to better stick to the chips, lightly paint the chips with some water and dip them in the spice mix, then let them dry). Serve.

Tip: Goes very well with the *Simple and Savory Guacamole* a few pages back!

Healthy Crispy Crackers

Makes around 20 crackers.

Ingredients:

½ cup. pumpkin seeds

½ cup. sesame seeds

½ cup. sunflower seeds

½ cup. chia seeds

1 cup. water

1 large garlic clove, finely grated

1 tsp. sweet onion, finely grated

¼ tsp. sea salt

Directions:

1. - Preheat your oven to 325ºF (160 ºC) and make ready a baking tray covered with bakery paper.

2. - Blend all the seeds together in a large bowl.

3. - Put the grated garlic and onion together with the water. Whisk it up.

4. - Pour the water mixture into the seed bowl and stir it well, until everything is combined.

5. - Season it with the sea salt (and any other spices and herbs you may want to include).

6. - Spread the blend onto the baking tray with a spoon until it's about ¼ inch thick.

7. - Bake at 325°F (160 °C) for 30 minutes. Remove the tray from the oven.

8. - Divide the blend into desired cracker shapes. Flip them around and bake with the other side up for another 30 minutes, or when the lower part acquires a golden tint.

9. - Let the crackers cool on the tray for a bit. Serve.

Spiced Potatoes and Sweet Potatoes

Makes 4 servings, recommended serving size 1 heaping cup.

Ingredients:

3 large Russet potatoes, peeled, sliced into thick matchsticks

1 large sweet potato, peeled, sliced into thick matchstick, (substitute taro, if desired)

1 small garlic bulb, top sliced off but keep bulb whole

1 bird's eye chili, stemmed, roughly chopped

⅛ tsp. dried rosemary or powdered rosemary

⅛ tsp. dried thyme or powdered thyme

1 pinch, generous kosher salt

1 pinch, generous black pepper

2 Tbsp. olive oil, for drizzling

Directions:

1. - Preheat oven to 350°F or 175°C for at least 10 minutes prior to use. Line a baking sheet with parchment paper.

2. - Place all ingredients in large mixing bowl. Toss well to combine. Put garlic bulb in the center of prepared baking sheet, sliced side up. Lay remaining vegetables flat on baking sheet to ensure even cooking.

3. - Bake these in hot oven for 45 minutes or until fork tender. If the potatoes and sweet potatoes are browning too fast, cover veggies with a sheet of aluminum foil and continue cooking.

4. - Remove baking sheet from oven and place on cooling rack. Let veggies cool slightly for easier handling.

5. - To serve: discard garlic bulb. Divide potatoes and sweet potatoes into 4 equal portions. Plate. Serve.

Deconstructed Pesto on Instant Sourdough Pizza

Makes 1 9-inch pizza, or 6 generous/8 smaller slices, recommended serving size is 1 slice.

Ingredients:

For "instant" sour dough:

1¼ cups bread flour, add more if needed

1 cup warm water

1 Tbsp. vinegar

1 Tbsp. olive oil, for greasing

1 tsp. kosher salt

1 tsp. instant yeast or quick rising yeast

¼ tsp. sugar

For pesto topping:

6 large basil leaves, julienned, add more for garnish if desired

1 large garlic clove, minced

1 pinch kosher salt

¼ cup pine nuts, freshly toasted on dry pan, roughly chopped, add more if desired

Extra virgin oil for topping

Black pepper, to taste

1 large fresh tomato, sliced paper-thin, drained well and pat-dried with paper towels, for garnish, optional

½ cup cashew cheese, optional

Directions:

1.. - <u>To make dough</u>: combine instant yeast, sugar and warm water in a small bowl. Whisk until frothy. Set aside for 10 to 15 minutes until bubbles form.

2. - Except for olive oil, place remaining ingredients into large mixing bowl. Mix. Make well in the center.

3. - Pour in yeast mixture. Mix until dough comes together, and turn out on lightly floured surface. Knead until it becomes smooth, and no longer sticks to your hands. Add more flour whenever needed. This would take 4 to 6 minutes.

4. - Drizzle small amount of oil into mixing bowl. Put dough inside, and lightly grease top. Cover bowl with saran wrap until ready to use. Divide into 2 equal portions.

Note: you can use dough as is, which will yield a crispy pizza crust. Or you can let dough rise once, punch down, and proof again in 2 hour intervals for a fluffier crust. This recipe only uses half portions of dough. Reserve the other half for other pizza, pita or *pierogi* recipes.

5. - <u>To assemble the pizza</u>: preheat oven to 430°F or 220°C. Lightly grease a 10-inch pizza tray with olive oil.

6. - Place half-portion of dough on pizza tray. Using your fingers and knuckles, stretch dough out so it covers entire surface of pizza tray.

7. - Spread garlic-salt mixture evenly on top of dough. Sprinkle basil leaves and pine nuts on top.

8. - Season well with olive oil and black pepper.

9. - Layer tomatoes on top, with dollops of cashew cheese in between, if using.

10. - Bake pizza for 8 to 10 minutes, or until crust becomes crisp.

11. - Remove pizza tray from oven and place on cooling rack for at least 3 minutes prior to slicing.

12. - Slice pizza into 6 generous portions or 8 smaller slices. Serve warm.

Squash Flower Pizza

Makes 1 9-inch pizza, or 6 generous/8 smaller slices, recommended serving size is 1 slice.

Ingredients:

½ **Instant Sourdough Pizza** dough, (see previous recipe)

For topping:

12 large squash flowers, use petals only, roughly torn, rinsed well, spun-dried

6 large asparagus spears, tough ends snapped off, sliced into 1-inch long slivers, rinsed, drained

1 can, 15 oz. button mushrooms, pieces and stems, rinsed well, drained

1 tsp. capers in brine, rinsed well, drained

¼ tsp. garlic salt, vegan-safe

Extra virgin oil for topping

Black pepper, to taste

¼ cup cashew cheese, optional

Directions:

1. - To assemble pizza: preheat oven to 430°F or 220°C. Lightly grease a 10-inch pizza tray with olive oil.

2. - Place dough on pizza tray. Using your fingers and knuckles, stretch dough out so it covers entire surface of pizza tray.

3. - Season dough with garlic salt.

4. - Layer on the asparagus slivers, button mushrooms and capers. Dollop cashew cheese, if using.

5. - Spread squash flowers on top and season well with olive oil and black pepper.

6. - Bake pizza for 8 to 10 minutes, or until flowers brown a little and crust crisps up.

7. - Remove pizza tray from oven and place on cooling rack for at least 3 minutes prior to slicing.

8. - Slice pizza into 6 generous portions or 8 smaller slices. Serve warm.

Cheesy Kale Chips

Makes 3-4 servings.

Ingredients:

2 garlic cloves

1 bunch curly kale, remove stems and break into smaller pieces

½ lemon, juiced

1/3 cup unsalted, raw cashews

¾ cup nutritional yeast

2 Tbsp. refined coconut oil or a vegetable oil

2 Tbsp. soy sauce

2 tsp. Dijon mustard

Directions:

1. - Preheat an oven to 200°F/95°C. Line 2 baking sheets with bakery paper.

2. - Blend coconut oil and cashews together in a food processor, until the mixture somewhat resembles peanut butter.

3. - Add the rest of the ingredients to the processor and blend them up, except for the kale.

4. - Combine the "cheesy" mixture with the kale pieces. Rub the mixture into kale leaves until each piece is sufficiently coated.

5. - Bake for 1 hour or until the kale is dry and crispy. Remove from the oven and serve.

Tip: Any leftovers can be kept in an airtight container for up to 5 days.

Spicy Roasted Chickpeas

Makes 1 cup of Spicy Roasted Chickpeas.

Ingredients:

1 cup chickpeas

1 tsp. olive oil

1 tsp. nutritional yeast

½ tsp. garlic powder

½ tsp. dried basil

½ tsp. red pepper flakes

¼ tsp cayenne pepper

¼ tsp. salt

Directions:

1. - Prepare a baking pan covered in aluminum foil.

2. - Preheat your oven to 450°F (230 °C).

3. - Drain and rinse the chickpeas, then dry them.

4. - Combine the chickpeas, oil and all of the seasonings in a small bowl. Mix well until the chickpeas are somewhat evenly coated.

5. - Pour the peas into the prepared baking pan. Shake the pan until the chickpeas are evened out to a single layer.

6. - Place the pan in the oven and roast at 450 °F (230 °C) for 10 minutes. Toss the chickpeas and roast for another 10 minutes, or until the peas are golden with a slight tint of brown.

7. - Let the chickpeas cool for around 30 minutes. Serve.

Easy Fluffy Vegan Rolls

Makes 10-12 servings.

Ingredients:

2 cups flour (keep some extra for kneading)

½ cup almond milk

¼ cup water

2 Tbsp. cane sugar

2 Tbsp. vegan butter

½ tsp. sea salt

2 ¼ tsp. instant yeast

Directions:

1. - Use a large bowl to combine the sugar, salt, yeast and ¾ cup of flour.

2. - In another, smaller bowl, mix the water, almond milk and vegan butter. Microwave this mixture for 50 seconds, or heat in a small saucepan until it is lukewarm.

3. - Combine the wet and dry ingredients and beat properly for around 2 minutes.

4. - Add ¼ cup of flour and beat for another 2 minutes. After this, add enough flour to make the dough soft.

5. - Place the dough on a lightly floured surface and knead until it's smooth. Then, let the dough rest for 10 minutes.

6. - Divide the dough into 10-12 pieces and roll them into ball shapes. Place them in a container.

7. - Cover the dough and let it rise in a temperate place for around 45 minutes.

8. - Preheat your oven to 375 ºF (190 ºC). Brush the top of the rolls with a thin layer of supplementary melted vegan butter.

9. - Bake for 18-20 minutes, or until the rolls look light golden brown and fluffy. Serve

Tip: Goes great with the Strawberry Flax Seed Jam in the *No-bake Sweets* section.

Spinach & Sesame Crackers

Makes 1 medium-sized bowl of crackers.

Ingredients:

2 cups spinach, fresh and washed

1 2/3 cups all-purpose flour

¼ cup water

1 Tbsp. white sesame seeds

1 Tbsp. olive oil

1 ½ tsp. baking powder

1 tsp. salt

Directions:

1. - Pre-heat your oven to 400°F (200°C).

2. - Put the spinach and the water into a blender. Blend until it is smooth.

3. - In a mixing bowl, combine the salt, baking powder, flour and sesame seeds. Whisk properly and then add in the blended spinach and water, as well as the olive oil.

4. - Mix the ingredients well, and knead with your hands until the dough becomes smooth. Add additional flour if the dough is too sticky.

5. - Prepare a floured baking sheet with bakery paper, and roll out the dough until it is evenly and thin.

6. - Cut the dough horizontally and vertically so that the dough is shaped into small squares.

7. - Bake in oven for around 20 minutes, or until crispy. Serve.

Tip: Goes very well with both the hummus and the guacamole in the *No-bake Savory Snacks* section!

"Veganism is not a sacrifice. It is a joy."
- Gary L. Francione

Printed in Great Britain
by Amazon.co.uk, Ltd.,
Marston Gate.